If you were an
Adjective

by Michael Dahl

illustrated by Sara Gray

PICTURE WINDOW BOOKS
Minneapolis, Minnesota

adjective (adj) a word that describes or modifies a noun or pronoun

Editor: Christianne Jones
Designer: Nathan Gassman
Page Production: Tracy Kaehler
Creative Director: Keith Griffin
Editorial Director: Carol Jones
The illustrations in this book were
created with acrylics.

Picture Window Books
5115 Excelsior Boulevard
Suite 232
Minneapolis, MN 55416
877-845-8392
www.picturewindowbooks.com

Library of Congress Cataloging-in-Publication Data
Dahl, Michael.
If you were an adjective / by Michael Dahl ;
illustrated by Sara Gray.
p. cm. — (Word fun)
Includes bibliographical references and index.
ISBN 1-4048-1356-X (hardcover)
1. English language—Adjective—Juvenile literature.
I. Gray, Sara, ill. II. Title. III. Series.
PE1241.D34 2006
428.1—dc22
2005021856

ISBN 1-4048-1982-7 (paperback)

Looking for adjectives? Watch for the big, colorful words in the example sentences.

Special thanks to our advisers for their expertise:
Rosemary G. Palmer, Ph.D., Department of Literacy
College of Education, Boise State University
Susan Kesselring, M.A., Literacy Educator
Rosemount–Apple Valley–Eagan (Minnesota) School District

If you were an adjective ...

3

... you
would be

4

COLORFUL!

BRILLIANT!

DAZZLING!

FEATHERY!

MANY-LEGGED!

SLIMY!

5

If you were an adjective, you would work side by side with nouns. A noun names a person, place, or thing. As an adjective, you would be busy describing nouns.

An elephant is a noun.

If you were an adjective, you would tell us about the elephant.

The **GRAY** elephant is **GIGANTIC** and **WET**. The SPARKLING water cools down the elephant.

If you were an adjective, you would tell us how a person, place, or thing looks.

The SLENDER swimmer snaps a photo of

the **ENORMOUS** whale in the **DEEP**, **BLUE** water.

If you were an adjective,
you would describe things.

The **TINY** kittens are **FLUFFY.**

The **LITTLE** piglets are **PUDGY** and **PINK.**

The **COLORFUL** peacock's tail is **BIG** and **BRIGHT**.

If you were an adjective, you would describe how something sounds.

The howler monkey is LOUD!

The boa's movement is SILENT.

The **QUIET** mouse
watches and waits.

If you were an adjective, you would describe how something feels.

The alligator's back is RIDGED and BUMPY.

15

If you were an adjective, you would describe how something behaves.

The **FEARLESS** plover is **CAREFUL** when it picks at the alligator's teeth.

If you were an adjective, you might be a proper adjective.

A proper adjective describes a specific object and is always capitalized.

In winter, the **Arctic** fox's coat turns white to blend in with the snow of the **Alaskan** tundra.

19

If you were an adjective, you could compare things. You would change your ending to show how things are different.

You would be a comparative adjective if you compared two things.

The turtle is **SMALL.**

The tree frog is **SMALLER.**

You would be a superlative adjective if you compared three things.

The lion is **FAST.**

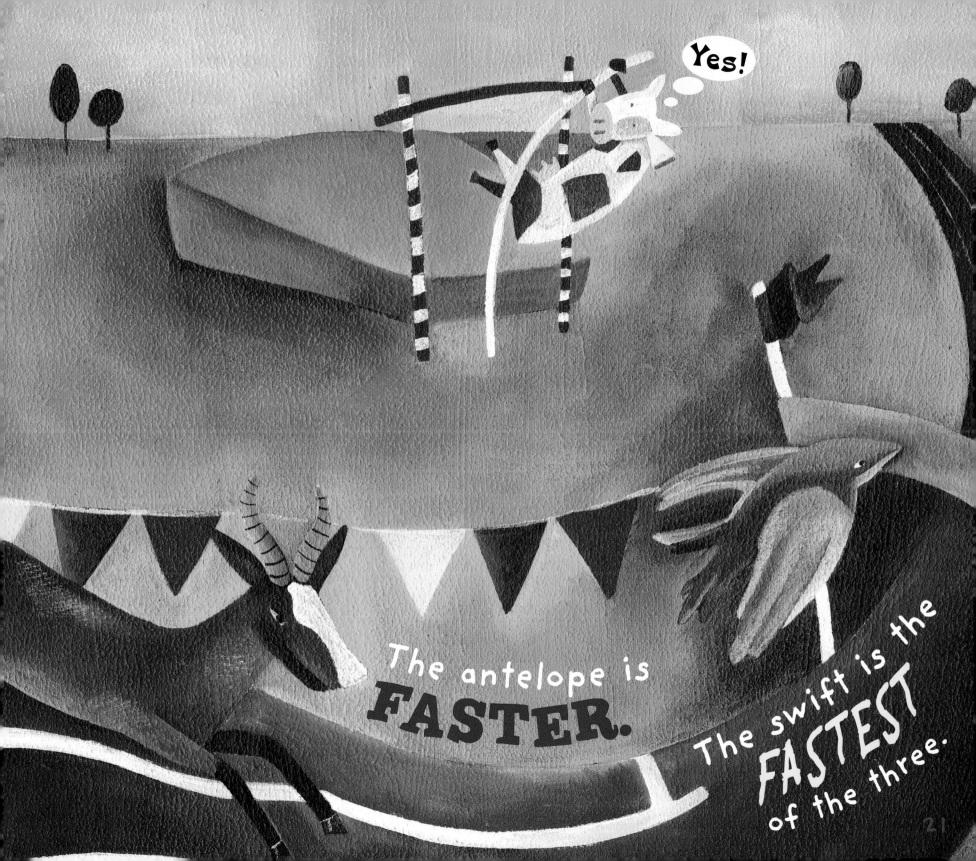

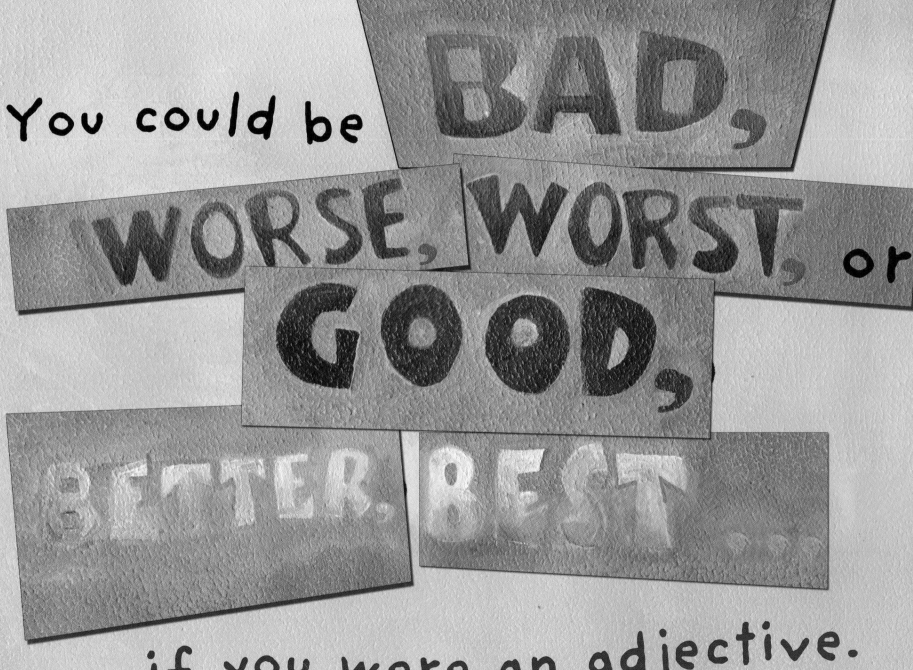

You could be BAD, WORSE, WORST, or GOOD, BETTER, BEST ...
... if you were an adjective.

Fun with Adjectives

Directions:
Write your name from top to bottom on a piece of paper. Now, think of adjectives that describe you. Use the letters in your name as the first letters of the adjectives. For example, you might write:

Mysterious
Intelligent
Creative
Happy
Athletic
Easy-going
Loud

Then, see if you can find adjectives to describe your friends

Fact: If you look up an adjective in the dictionary, you will see the abbreviation "adj" next to it. The "adj" stands for adjective.

Glossary

gigantic—huge

noun—a person, place, or thing

plover—a type of shorebird with a short, hard bill

pudgy—short and fat

ridged—bumpy

swift—a type of bird related to hummingbirds

tundra—an area of flat or rolling plains with no trees

To Learn More

At the Library

Cleary, Brian P. *Hairy, Scary, Ordinary: What Is an Adjective?* Minneapolis: Carolrhoda Books, 2000.

Doudna, Kelly. *Adjectives*. Edina, Minn.: Abdo Pub., 2001.

Heinrichs, Ann. *Adjectives*. Chanhassen, Minn.: Child's World, 2004.

On the Web

FactHound offers a safe, fun way to find Internet sites related to this book. All of the sites on FactHound have been researched by our staff.

1. Visit *www.facthound.com*
2. Type in this special code for age-appropriate sites: 140481356X
3. Click on the FETCH IT button.

Your trusty FactHound will fetch the best sites for you!

Look for all of the books in the Word Fun series:

If You Were a Noun
1-4048-1355-1

If You Were a Verb
1-4048-1354-3

If You Were an Adjective
1-4048-1356-X

If You Were an Adverb
1-4048-1357-8